CHILDREN OF THE TIPI
LIFE IN THE BUFFALO DAYS

EDITED BY
MICHAEL OREN FITZGERALD

❖ Wisdom Tales ❖

Children of the Tipi: Life in the Buffalo Days
©Wisdom Tales, 2013

Book Design by Stephen Williams

Wisdom Tales is an imprint of World Wisdom, Inc.

Library of Congress Cataloging-in-Publication Data

Children of the tipi : life in the buffalo days / edited by Michael Oren Fitzgerald.
    pages cm.
  ISBN 978-1-937786-09-0 (hardcover : alk. paper) 1. Indians of North America--Great Plains--History--Juvenile
literature. 2. Indians of North America--Great Plains--Social life and customs--Juvenile literature. I. Fitzgerald,
Michael Oren, 1949-
  E78.G73C53 2013
  978.004'97--dc23

                                                                    2013001789

Printed in China on acid-free paper

Production Date: February, 2013; Plant & Location: Printed by Everbest Printing
(Guangzhou, China), Co., Ltd.; Job / Batch # : 111390

For information address Wisdom Tales, P.O. Box 2682, Bloomington, Indiana 47402-2682
www.wisdomtalespress.com

EDITOR'S NOTE

❖ How can our children understand the essential character of the nomadic American Indians of the nineteenth century?

❖ What lessons can our young ones learn from the Native Americans about virgin Nature?

They can learn the wisdom of the olden-day Indians directly from the source. Even though the nomads of the plains and forests have long since vanished, we can still glimpse the spirit of that irreplaceable world directly through their words and photographs.

Children of the Tipi introduces us to the wisdom of the foremost members of many American Indian tribes. All the quotes are from men and women born before 1904.* Most of them lived in the nomadic days before reservations or are the children who learned by listening to stories at the feet of these "old-timers."

The majority of these photographs are rare. Most of them are taken from several thousand photographs that I have collected over almost forty years, including research done in the Library of Congress in 1974. All of the photographs ever submitted for copyright protection are in that facility, and at that time it was still possible to roam freely through the stacks and to easily obtain copies of those photographs whose copyright protection had expired.

These pages have a certain focus on the Plains Indians because they were the last group of tribes to resist the white encroachment. Their material culture was the best documented of all American Indian tribes. When considering Native wisdom, it is evident that there are many variations among the tribes. However, few will deny that there are unifying themes, including the emphasis they placed on moral character and the sacred quality of virgin Nature. This book focuses on those common themes.

In today's fast-paced world, we often lose our connection to teachings of sacred value that can provide a stabilizing response to the challenges which we encounter on a daily basis. It is my hope that the insights conveyed in *Children of the Tipi* will help our children to better understand the sacred spirit that dwells in every person so they are better prepared to meet the challenges of life.

Michael Fitzgerald
September, 2012

* I have edited several of the quotes for young readers. The original quotes are presented in two of my other books: *The Spirit of Indian Women* and *Indian Spirit: Revised and Enlarged.*

MOTHERS

The heart of the family is the mother.
Life comes from her.
—Onondaga Proverb

papoose

Women have power: Children.
Can any warrior make a child,
no matter how brave and
wonderful he is?
—Maria Chona, Papago

It is the mothers, not the warriors, who create a people and guide their destiny.
—Standing Bear, Oglala Lakota

moccasins

A nation is not conquered until the hearts of its women are on the ground. Then, no matter how brave its warriors nor how strong their weapons, it is done.
—Cheyenne Proverb

HOW CHILDREN GOT THEIR NAMES

The Crow people used a name blessing to bring good health and prosperity to the child. They invited an outstanding warrior to give the name blessing. After the ceremony the father invited his clan brothers to a feast. An Indian name is still considered important to the health and the success of Crow children.
—Agnes Yellowtail Deernose, Absaroke

toy tipis

Sioux toy horse

GIRLS AT PLAY

toy doll
in cradle
board

toy dolls

My mother and aunt gathered an abundant
supply of corn. I was left to watch the corn
dry. I played around it with dolls made of
ears of corn. I braided the soft fine corn silk
for hair. The dolls had blankets from scraps
I found in my mother's workbag.
—Zitkala-Ša, Lakota

BOYS LOVE BOWS AND ARROWS

Our games were feats with the bow and arrow. We had foot and pony races, wrestling and swimming. We imitated the customs and habits of our fathers.
—Charles Eastman (Ohiyesa), Wahpeton Dakota

the bow and arrow game

The first gift I received from my father was a bow and arrows. He made them himself. He painted the bow red, which signified that he had been wounded in battle. I was very young at the time, so the arrows were fashioned with knobs on the end, instead of the sharp points. The bow was not a strong one to pull. That bow and arrows was the beginning of my Indian training. It was to be my weapon in war, and was to get my food for me. I always kept it near me.
—Standing Bear, Oglala Lakota

Always At Play...

My people teach their children never to make fun of any one. If you see your brother or sister doing something wrong, then go away from them. If you make fun of bad persons, you make yourself beneath them. Be kind to all, both poor and rich. Feed all that come to your wigwam. In this way you will make many friends. Your name will be honored far and near. This is the way my people teach their children. It was handed down from father to son for many generations.
—Sarah Winnemucca, Piute

The girls usually decided where the play village was to be located. Some boys had thier own ponies and we had play attacks on the camp. This was lots of fun. Some of the girls had their dolls in little carriers, and they would run. The boys on their side would fight us. If a boy fell off his pony while in the camp of the enemy, one of us would be brave and try to rescue him. It was just like the stories which were told to us at home. There was no roughness shown among the children. We always "played fair," as we were taught to be fair in all things.
—Standing Bear, Oglala Lakota

...Even In The Snow

When you see a new trail you do not know,
follow it to the point of knowing.
—Uncheedah, Dakota

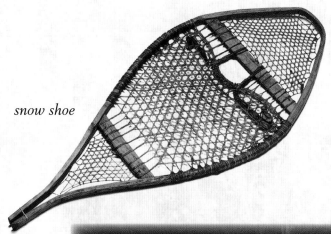

snow shoe

We had play fights with mud balls and
willow wands. In summer we played lacrosse.
In winter we coasted upon the ribs of
animals and buffalo robes.
—Charles Eastman (Ohiyesa), Wahpeton
Dakota

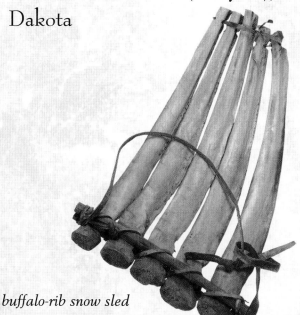

buffalo-rib snow sled

GRANDMOTHERS

Indian people loved their children above all else. They were a special gift from the Creator. They were the promise of a bright and happy future. They particularly spent time with their grandparents. Their parents were often too busy working to give them the full attention they deserved. Grandparents devoted time to their care and wisdom to pass on to the next generation. Our most important sense of self and education came from the very old. They were so kind, gentle, considerate, and wise with us.
—Mourning Dove, Salish

shell necklace

As a child, I often fell asleep while my grandmother told me a story or sang a song. Thinking of these legends brings back the old days so vividly. People should imagine themselves in a tipi, with the firelight throwing light and shadow on the eager listening faces. The fire seemed to sympathize and keep pace with the story. We had only these legends and stories in place of your science and literature.

—Bright Eyes (Susette LaFlesche), Omaha

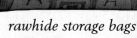

rawhide storage bags

girl's dress

13

Story-Telling

headdress

Kids learned just through listening and watching. Then they tried. Our folks didn't lecture us much. They told stories, especially on the long winter nights. We listened and learned what to fear, what to do, and what to respect.
—Agnes Yellowtail Deernose, Absaroke

I loved best the evening meal, for that was the time old legends were told. I ate my supper in quiet, listening to the old people. As each began to tell a legend, I laid my head on my mother's lap. Then the increasing interest of the tale aroused me. I sat up and eagerly listened to every word. The old women made funny remarks and everyone joined them in hearty laughter.
—Zitkala-Ša, Lakota

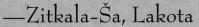

MOTHER EARTH

The Lakota loved the earth and all things of the earth. The old people came to love the soil. They sat on the ground to be close to a mothering power. It was good for the skin to touch the earth. The old people liked to remove their moccasins and walk with bare feet on the sacred earth.

The old Lakota was wise. He knew that man's heart away from nature becomes hard. He knew that lack of respect for growing, living things led to lack of respect for humans. So he kept his youth close to nature.

—Standing Bear, Oglala Lakota

Nomadic Life

dog travois

A crier would ride through the village telling the people to be ready to move in the morning. In every lodge the children's eyes would shine. Long before the sun came up, hundreds of horses came thundering in. Down came the lodges and the travois loaded. Ho! Away we would go to a new camping ground. On the way our children played around us. It was good hard work.

Ahh, my people were tough in those days. Now, when people get wet they build a fire to get dry again. Now, my people wear gloves and too many clothes. We are soft as mud.

—Pretty Shield, Absaroke

When I was young, I heard people talk about the old times. They said it was good when they camped and roamed on the plains. I think about the way I used to live, when we gathered berries and wild food. We ate rabbits, grouse, porcupine, and beaver. It was a good life. We ate everything and it made us strong. No one was toothless. No one got discouraged or was lazy. No one drank hard liquor or fought one another.

Life is so different now. No one wants to live in the country anymore. There are even some people today that always lived in town. They will never know what it was like to live in the country.

—Belle Highwalking, Northern Cheyenne

horse travois

Daily Camp Life

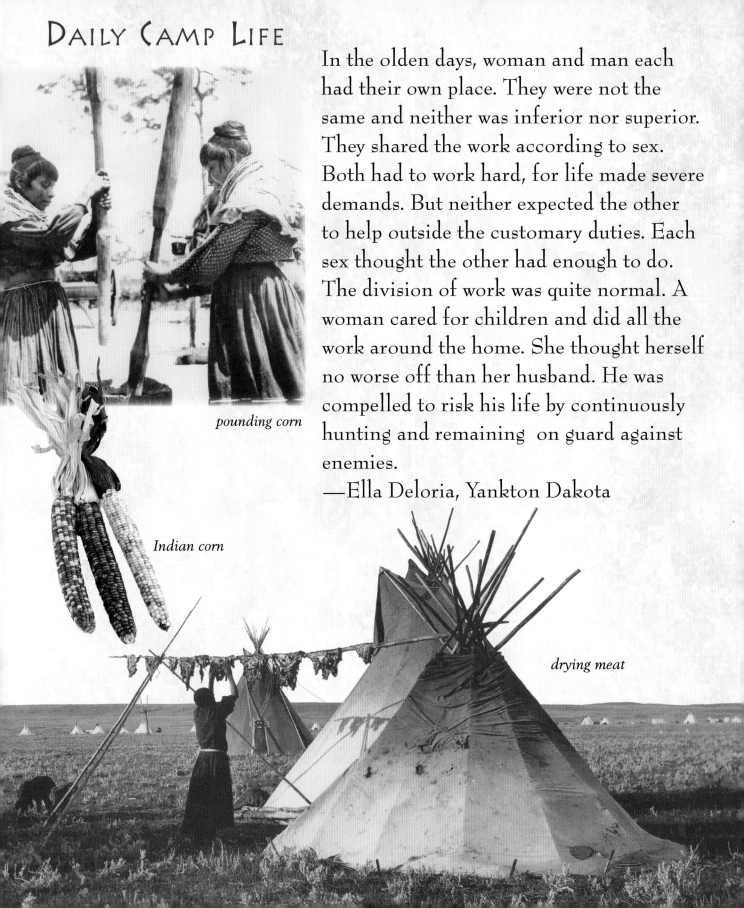

In the olden days, woman and man each had their own place. They were not the same and neither was inferior nor superior. They shared the work according to sex. Both had to work hard, for life made severe demands. But neither expected the other to help outside the customary duties. Each sex thought the other had enough to do. The division of work was quite normal. A woman cared for children and did all the work around the home. She thought herself no worse off than her husband. He was compelled to risk his life by continuously hunting and remaining on guard against enemies.

—Ella Deloria, Yankton Dakota

pounding corn

Indian corn

drying meat

wooden bowl

buffalo horn spoon

I always made my morning prayer on the mesa's edge with mother, cousins and aunts. First, we breathed on the corn meal in our hands. Then, we prayed for long life and good health. Next, we tossed the meal into the spirit world toward the rising sun. As the first rays of the sun slid over the horizon, we reached out and symbolically pressed the beams to our bodies. We prayed that we might be beautiful in body, face, and heart. This protected us from evil. Then we had the strength to meet the day and its problems.

—Polingaysi Qoyawayma (Elizabeth White), Hopi

Cooking meat with heated stones in a buffalo-stomach container

making turquoise jewelry

making pottery

Navajo weaver

In weaving, painting, and use of beads and quills the red man had an excellent color sense. The women did most of this work. They displayed vast skill in selecting materials and dyes. A variety of beautiful grasses, roots, and barks are used for baskets by the different tribes. Some used gorgeous feathers for extra ornamentation. Each was perfectly adapted in style, size, and form.
—Charles Eastman (Ohiyesa), Wahpeton Dakota

Music and Dance

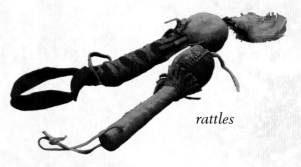

rattles

The Hopi way has a strong but invisible web, holding the people together. We express ourselves through our ritual dances and songs. They have been handed down from generation to generation. In all things, great and small, the true Hopi saw the forces of creation. This spiritual understanding gave a sense of depth and dignity to our often difficult everyday existence. The young people respected the wisdom of our elders. The devotion of the elders provided the children with mental and spiritual education.
—Polingaysi Qoyawayma, Hopi

flutes

drum and stick

I add my breath to your breath;
That our days may be long on the Earth;
That the days of our people may be long;
That we may be one person;
That we may finish our roads together;
May our Mother Earth bless you with life;
May our life paths be fulfilled.
—Wedding Song of Laguna Pueblo

23

TIPIS

painted tipis

Sacred support was always present for traditional Indians. From the moment you arose and said your first prayer, you could see what was necessary in order to lead a proper life. Even the dress that you wore had sacred meanings.

You carried a sense of the sacred with you. All of the forms had meaning, even the tipi and the sacred circle of the entire camp. Of course, the life was hard and difficult. And, not all Indians followed the rules. But the traditional life and the presence of Nature brought great blessings on all the people.

—Yellowtail, Absaroke

MEN HUNTED FAR FROM CAMP...

When I was nine years old, my grandfather made me a bow and arrows. I hunted rabbits, prairie dogs, and prairie chickens. I became an excellent marksman and added to our food supply.
—Fools Crow, Lakota

quiver and arrows

stone arrowheads

woven baskets

harvesting fruit

Children were encouraged to develop strict discipline. They had a high regard for sharing. When a girl picked her first berries and dug her first roots, she gave them away to an elder. When a child carried water for the home, an elder gave compliments. The child was encouraged not to be lazy and to grow straight like a sapling.

—Mourning Dove, Salish

picking berries

A Sacred Way Of Life

Traditional Indians did not depend on someone else to do their work. Nor, did they depend on someone else to say their prayers. Every day, in whatever they did, they lived in a sacred manner. Each of these things may seem small. But, it is a series of small things that make up our lives.
—Yellowtail, Absaroke

pipe bag

eagle bone whistle

pipe

The Great Spirit is everywhere. He hears whatever is in our minds and hearts. And, it is not necessary to speak to Him in a loud voice.
—Black Elk, Oglala Lakota

Whenever the red hunter comes upon a scene that is strikingly beautiful, he pauses for an instant in the attitude of worship. He sees no need for setting apart one day in seven as a holy day. To him all days are God's.
—Charles Eastman (Ohiyesa), Wahpeton Dakota

HORSES

There were many ways we boys trained ponies. One way was to drive the wild ponies into deep water, swim up to them, and play with them. Horses in the water cannot kick hard, so there was little danger of getting hurt. We would not be rough with the animals. We would play with them until they were used to us. Then they could see we would not harm them. After a while we climbed on their backs. They didn't seem to mind at all.

None of the methods we used to train ponies were hard on the animal. A pony trained with kindness makes a finer and more trustworthy animal than one broken through abuse. As we grew up to manhood, they grew up to horsehood. They understood us as well as we understood them.
—Standing Bear, Oglala Lakota

saddles

saddle blanket

Of all the animals the horse is the Indian's best friend, for without it he could not go on long journeys. A horse is the Indian's most valuable possession.
—Brave Buffalo, Lakota

riding whip

Living In Nature

We should understand that all things are the work of the Great Spirit. He is within all things: the trees, the rivers, the mountains, and all the animals. He is also above all these things and peoples. When we understand all this deeply in our hearts, then we will fear, and love, and know the Great Spirit. Then we will act and live as He intends.
—Black Elk, Oglala Lakota

Look at the sun, the moon, and the stars in the sky. Look at the changing seasons. Look at the ripening fruits of spring. Anyone must realize that all this is the work of someone more powerful than man.
—Chased by Bears, Yanktonai Dakota

The land was put here by the Great Spirit. We cannot sell it because it does not belong to us. You can count your money and burn it within the nod of a buffalo's head. But only the Great Spirit can count the grains of sand and the blades of grass.

As a present to you, we will give you anything that you can take with you. But we will never sell the land. Never.
—A Blackfeet Chief

eagle feather necklace

eagle headdress

lance

Great Chiefs

The truly brave man yields neither to fear nor anger, desire nor agony. He is at all times master of himself.
—Charles Eastman (Ohiyesa), Wahpeton Dakota

As a Nez Perce man passed through the forest, the moving trees whispered to him. His heart heard the song of the swaying pine. He felt the song of the clouds. Each bird spoke its message to his heart.
—Chief Joseph, Nez Perce

Chief Joseph, Nez Perce

All the Indians pray to God for life. We try to find out a good road, and do nothing wrong in this life. This is what we want. You should say nothing against our religion. We say nothing against yours. You pray to God. So do all of us Indians. We both pray to only one God, who made us all.
—Sitting Bull, Hunkpapa Lakota

Sitting Bull, Lakota

tomahawk

knife sheath

Chief Medicine Crow, Absaroke

35

coup stick

Sell a country! Why not sell the air, the clouds, and the great sea? Why not sell the earth? The Great Spirit made them all for the use of His children.
—Tecumseh (Shooting Star), Shawnee

Civilized people depend too much on man-made printed pages. I turn to the Great Spirit's book, which is the whole of His creation. You can read a big part of that book if you study nature. Take all your books, lay them out under the sun and let the snow, the rain, and insects work on them. There will be nothing left. But the Great Spirit provided you and me with an opportunity for study in nature's university. Look at the forests, the rivers, the mountains, and the animals, which include us.

—Walking Buffalo, Stoney

shield

Remember that your children are
not your own. They are lent to
you by the Creator.
—Mohawk Proverb

The Great Spirit does not make two birds, or animals, or human beings exactly alike. Each is placed here by the Great Spirit to be independent and to rely on itself.
—Shooter, Lakota

The grandfathers and the grandmothers are in the children. Teach them well.
—Ojibwa Proverb

About Michael Oren Fitzgerald

Michael Fitzgerald has authored or edited over fifteen books which have received in excess of two dozen awards, including the prestigious ForeWord Book of the Year Award, the Ben Franklin Award, and the USA Best Books Award.

More than ten of Michael's books, along with two documentary films he produced, are used in high-school or university classes. He previously taught the Religious Traditions of the North American Indians at Indiana University.

He is an adopted son of the late Thomas Yellowtail, one of the most honored American Indian spiritual leaders of the last century.

Michael and his wife, award-winning editor and designer, Judith Fitzgerald, live in southern Indiana close to their grandchilden, who are at the root of their desire to produce quality books for children and young adults.

American Indian Books by Judith & Michael Oren Fitzgerald

The Spirit of Indian Women, World Wisdom, 2005

Indian Spirit: Revised & Enlarged, World Wisdom, 2006

American Indian Books Written & Edited by Michael Oren Fitzgerald

Yellowtail: Crow Medicine Man and Sun Dance Chief, University of Oklahoma Press, 1991

The Essential Charles Eastman (Ohiyesa): Light on the Indian World, World Wisdom, 2002, Revised 2007

Native Spirit: The Sun Dance Way, by Thomas Yellowtail, World Wisdom, 2007

The Spiritual Legacy of the American Indian, by Joseph Epes Brown, World Wisdom, 2007

Living in Two Worlds: The American Indian Experience, by Charles Eastman, World Wisdom, 2010

American Indian Films Produced by Michael Oren Fitzgerald

The Sun Dance Way, World Wisdom, 2006

Native Spirit, World Wisdom, 2007

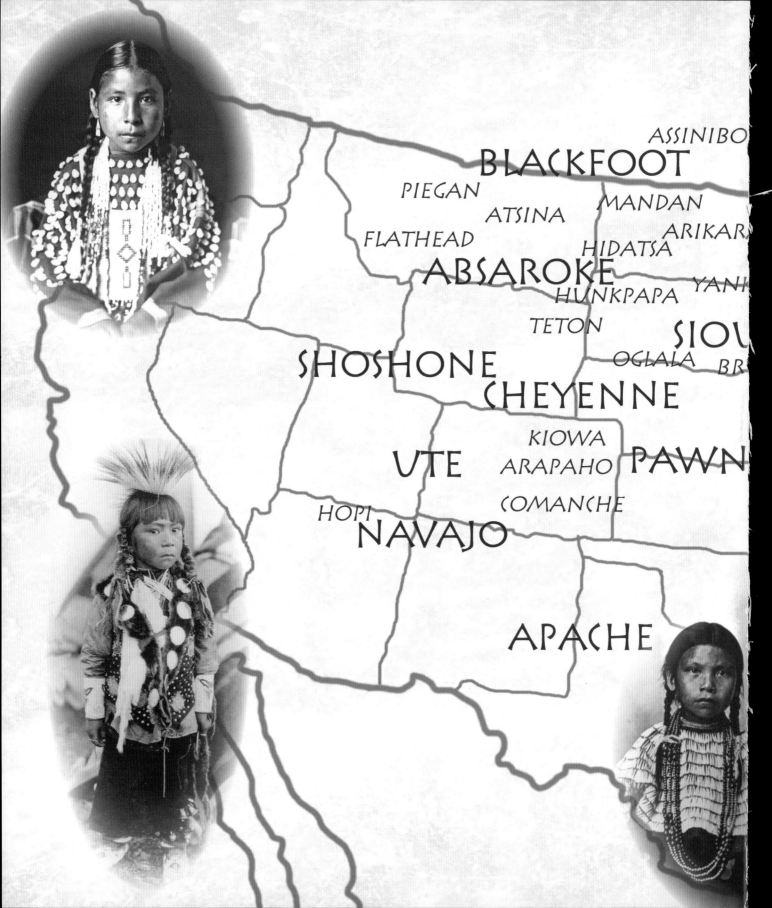

ASSINIBO

BLACKFOOT

PIEGAN

ATSINA

MANDAN

FLATHEAD

ARIKAR

HIDATSA

ABSAROKE

YANK

HUNKPAPA

TETON

SIOU

SHOSHONE

OGLALA   BR

CHEYENNE

KIOWA

UTE

ARAPAHO

PAWN

COMANCHE

HOPI

NAVAJO

APACHE